Hard Wor

# A Day with a Mechanic

## By Joanne Winne

Welcome Books

Children's Press
A Division of Grolier Publishing
New York / London / Hong Kong / Sydney
Danbury, Connecticut

Photo Credits: Cover and all photos by Maura Boruchow
Contributing Editor: Jeri Cipriano
Book Design: Michael DeLisio

# Contents

1   Meet a Mechanic     4

2   Adding Oil     10

3   Checking the Water     12

4   Taking off a Tire     16

5   New Words     22

6   To Find Out More     23

7   Index     24

8   About the Author     24

My name is Theresa.

I am a **mechanic**.

My job is to fix cars.

4

These cars are not working.

I check the cars to see what needs to be fixed.

7

Here is a car to fix.

First, I raise the **hood**.

9

Next, I add oil to
the **engine**.

The engine needs oil
to help it run.

Then, I check the water.

An engine needs water
to stay cool.

13

This car is on a **lift**.

I use the lift to raise the car.

The lift makes it easy for me to work.

14

15

This car needs a new **tire**.

I take off the old tire.

I will put on a new tire.

17

This car's back light is not working.

I put in a new **bulb**.

19

A mechanic has a busy job.

There are many parts of a car to fix.

I like being a mechanic.

21

# New Words

**bulb** (**bulb**) an object that gives off light

**engine** (**en**-jin) a machine that makes a car run

**hood** (**hud**) a piece of metal that covers the engine of a car

**lift** (**lift**) a machine that raises a car

**mechanic** (meh-**kan**-ik) a person who fixes cars

**tire** (**tyr**) a piece of rubber filled with air that goes around car wheels

# To Find Out More

**Books**
*An Auto Mechanic*
by Douglas Florian
William Morrow & Company

*At the Auto Repair Center*
by Justine Korman
Cartwheel Books

**Web Site**
**Automotive Learning Online**
http://www.innerauto.com/innerauto/htm/auto.html
Click on the picture of the car to find out its parts
and how these parts work.

# Index

bulb, 18

engine, 10, 12

hood, 8

lift, 14

mechanic, 4, 20

tire, 16

**About the Author**
Joanne Winne taught fourth grade for nine years. She currently writes and edits books for children. She lives in Hoboken, New Jersey.

**Reading Consultants**
Kris Flynn, Coordinator, Small School District Literacy, The San Diego County Office of Education

Shelly Forys, Certified Reading Recovery Specialist, W.J. Zahnow Elementary School, Waterloo, IL

Peggy McNamara, Professor, Bank Street College of Education, Reading and Literacy Program